Girl,

Get your Man!

FIVE EASY STEPS TO GET YOUR MAN
AND GET HIM TO COMMIT

I0173642

BILLIE HAWKINS

ISBN: 978-0-9883374-3-5

Cover Design: Brittany J. Jackson

Published by G Publishing, LLC

Printed in the United States of America

TABLE OF CONTENTS

INTRODUCTION

This book was written for all the single ladies, no matter the age, who are either looking for a committed relationship or marriage.

Listening to such comments from friends and acquaintances such as, "Girl, where are all the good men, or why won't he commit, or why can't I find a man?", inspired me to write this book.

This book is also for the single ladies who just want to step up their dating game.

Hopefully, this book will encourage all the single ladies to keep on trying and to not give up their quest for a committed relationship or marriage. It's not brain surgery, ladies. It's just common sense. Use what you have to get what you want!

STEP 1: GO WHERE THE MEN ARE

Attend church. Not only your church but others. You probably know most of the men at your church so branch out and reach out to other churches.

Go to sporting events, such as baseball games, basketball games, football games, etc. Join a fitness gym. Join groups that have a large male membership, such as political groups.

Attend dances, clubs, and parties. Give your own parties and invite eligible men that you like.

A recent poll showed that Home Depot is

a good place to meet men.

Have lunch or dinner at a restaurant frequented by a lot of men and don't be afraid to dine alone. You might be approached by someone.

Let others help you. Don't be afraid to let it be known that you are open to meeting someone. Your female friends have brothers, cousins, uncles, etc.

Avoid traveling with a lot of female friends or attending too many all-female events, if you are truly looking for a man.

If you are open to meeting other ethnicities, go where they are. Sometimes it pays to broaden ones options. Attend an interracial church event.

In this day and age, many use the internet to meet people. If this is an option for you, fine, but be careful. Don't wait too long to meet in person and meet during the day in a safe place where there are other people. Definitely do not meet at your home until you know him better.

The bottom line is, don't sit at home waiting for the phone to ring. Take a class, preferably one with men in it. Keep yourself looking good and <u>get out there!</u>

STEP 2: BE APPROACHABLE AND SMILE

No matter how well dressed you are, how nice your hair looks, or how carefully you have applied your makeup, if you are not sending out an approachable vibe, chances are you won't be approached. A smile goes a long way.

Many men are intimidated by attractive women and may want to approach you but are afraid of being rejected. That is why it is so important to smile and not send out a cold vibe. In fact, don't always wait for a man to approach <u>you</u>. If you see someone you're attracted to, approach <u>him.</u>

Example: "Hello, how are you? My name is _____. What's your name?" That will break the ice and you can then have a conversation

If you see a wedding ring, move on. If you don't, ask the question, "Are you married?" If he's single, continue the conversation. He might ask for your phone number. If he doesn't and you're interested in him, ask for his. That would be the greatest form of flattery for many men.

If someone approaches you and asks for your phone number and you're not particularly interested in him, tell him to give you his number, and you'll call him.

That way he doesn't feel rejected and you'll have control of the situation and can either call him or not.

Many ladies miss out on a good man because they are all about the superficial. They are looking for a certain "type". He must be tall, well built, have a full head of hair, etc.

Your chances of getting a good man will be greater if you are less judgmental.

Be as interested in what's on the inside as you are in what's on the outside, such as, does he have a good heart? Is he kind? Is he dependable? Is he into you as much as you are into him?

Also, perfecting the art of flirting will increase your chances of meeting a man. If you see a man you're interested in, let him catch you looking at him and smiling two or three times. Look at him, smile, and then look away. This sends out a vibe that you are interested and he'll probably come over and talk to you.

Keep up to date on current events and learn something about sports and learn to ask a lot of questions. That will keep the conversation going.

Have you ever seen a very good looking man with a woman who is, in your opinion, not that attractive, and wondered, "What does he see in her?"

Billie Hawkins

In talking to one of my male friends about this, he said something which I thought was very profound. He said that the woman probably had a wonderful personality, and a great sense of humor but the number one reason he was with her was because of the way she made him feel! He felt appreciated and loved.

So remember ladies, it's not always all about you.

If you really want a man, go where the men are. Keep yourself looking good, be real, and be kind and caring. Be fun to be with, be complimentary, be approachable, smile, flirt a little bit and it won't be long before you'll have the man you want. And

when you find him, make him feel like a
king.

Billie Hawkins

STEP 3: GET TO KNOW HIM

Once you have landed that first date, use it and subsequent dates to really get to know him.

There are many places one can go on a first date. I highly recommend a dinner date, where you can dress to impress, and also where you can have a meaningful conversation.

16   Billie Hawkins

Ask general questions on the first date like, where do you work? If unemployed, why? Have you ever been married? Do you have children? What are your hobbies-interests? Talk about current events and keep the conversation light. Compliment him on something, his voice, sense of humor, the tie he's wearing, etc. Let him know by your attitude that you like him. Be warm and inviting.

At the end of the date, tell him how much you enjoyed his company and that you'd really like to see him again, and if he doesn't give you a goodnight kiss, you give him one. You can't be coy. You must be proactive!

As things progress and you continue to date, here are some other questions you should be asking. What is your religion? Do you attend church? What are your short term goals? What are your long term goals? Do you see marriage and children in your future?

Find out his values by discussing various subjects and how he feels about certain things. Introduce him to family members and if you are really getting serious, now would be a good time to plan an activity that includes the children if you have any. Watch how they interact and be sure that he is respectful to them and they to him.

Also, when considering him as husband

material, don't rule him out because he is not where you'd like him to be financially. Consider his potential. Does he have a goal, a plan? Is he working toward his goal? If so, encourage him.

After all, the First Lady, Michelle Obama, took a chance on Barack Obama, who was a community organizer, driving an old beat-up car, when they started dating, and now he's the President of the United States! So, ladies, give a brother a chance.

When you are ready to take your relationship to the next level, do practice SAFE SEX! And remember, having sex doesn't mean you are in a committed relationship. You have to ask for what you want.

STEP 4: ASK FOR WHAT YOU WANT

Do you want a committed relationship? Ask for it. Do you want to get married? Ask for it.

I know a few couples who lived together before marriage and are now happily married; however, in my opinion, if you want to get married, do not move in with him!

You can see each other as often as you like, but don't move in together. If you do, that is one less incentive for him to marry you. Why get married? You are already playing house and that works for him.

If a committed relationship is what you want, in which he is dating you exclusively, don't hesitate to ask for it.

But if you really want to get married, let him know that you truly love him and want to be his wife. If he concurs, set a date. If he keeps putting it off and making excuses, give him an ultimatum.

He can either step up or step. If he really loves you and doesn't want to lose you, he'll step up. If he doesn't, it's time for you to step back and end the relationship before wasting any more time on him.

Oh sure, it will hurt for a while, but it will free you up so that you can find someone who will marry you. He is out there somewhere. You just have to be proactive and keep on looking.

And girls, when a man tells you that he doesn't want a committed relationship, or he doesn't want to get married, believe him! Stop trying to change his mind. He's not ready and you're just wasting your time. Move on!

Remember, the squeaking wheel gets the oil. Don't sit back waiting for something to happen. Anything worth having is worth working for. Be Flirty, be fun, be fearless! Girl, go get your man!

STEP 5: SEAL THE DEAL

Once you both have agreed to get married, set the date and start planning.

During this engagement period, get to know your respective families better, continue to keep up your physical appearance and continue being pleasant and fun to be with. Continue letting him know that you love and care for him and that you need and want him in your life, and on your wedding day, SEAL THE DEAL!

Billie Hawkins

WAYS TO MEET MEN

1. Join a political group and or work on a political campaign.

2. Join a singles group or start one yourself.

3. Ask friends and acquaintances to introduce you to available men.

4. Dine alone at restaurants occasionally. You might be approached by a man.

5. Take a class that's popular with men.

6. Learn to play golf (there are many men on golf courses)

7. If you want to meet senior men, join a senior center and participate

in their activities. Also, get to know the senior men in your church who are single and or widowed.

8. Invite a man that you like out to lunch or breakfast (your treat) and hope that he'll reciprocate. Don't always wait for the man to initiate.

PLACES TO MEET MEN

1. Churches

2. Grocery stores

3. Home depot

4. Weddings

5. Clubs

6. Parties

7. Concerts

8. Sporting events

9. Fitness gyms

10. Dances

11. Work

12. The Internet Dating Sites

ABOUT THE AUTHOR

Billie Hawkins is the author of What's Love Got To Do With It? Relationships 101, a book of short stories and poems about relationships.

She is a graduate of the Detroit Public Schools and Wayne State University and she is a former teacher. Her poetry has been published in three poetry anthologies and in the Wayne State Alumni Magazine. She is a storyteller, actress and performance poet and she enjoys giving relationship advice to friends and acquaintances.